TOTAL GUITAR

TECHNIQUE

Practice Skills

ESSENTIAL LESSONS & PLAYING MECHANICS

LUKE ZECCHIN

Getting lost on the guitar neck?
Finally, fretboard memorization made easy!

If you like this book, you'll love our *Fretboard Memorization Workshop*! This online master class is your shortcut to demystifying the fretboard puzzle. Here you'll be guided step-by-step through the key concepts, techniques, and exercises needed to master your entire fretboard—quickly and easily. These insights have helped thousands of students worldwide, and we're certain they'll help you too!

For more information, head to **LearnYourFretboard.com**.

This book is dedicated to all who endure those solitary hours in the practice room, long days on the tour bus, and late nights at the recording studio.

Published by **GuitarIQ.com**

Copyedited by Allister Thompson

Proofread by Dan Foster

Illustrated by Jasmin Zecchin

The author and publisher have made every effort to ensure the information contained in this book is both relevant and accurate at the time of release. They accept no responsibility for any loss, injury, or inconvenience sustained by any person using this book or the information provided within it.

Please Note: This guide was written to help improve your guitar playing technique. It isn't intended as a substitute for any form of medical diagnosis, treatment, or therapy. The information provided in this handbook in no way constitutes professional medical advice. If you experience consistent pain or regular discomfort when playing guitar, please seek the advice of a qualified medical professional who can assist you personally with this issue.

Contents

Get Your Free Online Bonus Now!

This book comes complete with free online bonus material. We've compiled a companion website to enhance your reading experience. Extras include audio examples, backing tracks, bonus downloads, and more!

Get your free bonus content at: **www.guitariq.com/tgt-bonus**

Preface

Welcome, and thank you for choosing *Total Guitar Technique*.

When we begin learning guitar, the emphasis is often on *what* we do—not *how* we do it. We focus on learning new patterns, playing the right notes, avoiding the wrong notes, and trying to keep it all in time. Foundational concepts like body position, relaxed movement, and efficiency of motion are commonly overlooked in the battle to just get our fingers to go where we want them!

The good news is, with some practice and persistence, what seemed so difficult at first becomes much easier. This initial struggle to produce something that sounded even vaguely musical slowly fades. The bad news is, the counterproductive playing habits we develop along the way don't disappear so easily. Playing tendencies that we learn early on become the framework for everything we do on guitar. From the way we position our body to the mechanics of moving our hands, it's very difficult to play with accuracy, speed, and consistency when our basic technique works against us.

This handbook is a combination of personal experience, trial and error, observation, and study from more than 20 years of guitar playing. The further your playing advances, the more you realize that *how* you do something directly impacts what you can do. Even experienced guitar players can encounter all kinds of basic issues, simply because they've learned to view their limiting playing habits as normal.

In this book, you'll find no flashy licks, playing tricks, or other so-called guitar "secrets." Instead, you'll find something much more valuable: the essential tools needed to unlock your full playing potential. Through this collection of exercises, concepts, and strategies, together we'll explore the key aspects of developing great playing technique. This guide isn't intended to be prescriptive. It isn't a rulebook or an attempt to develop a single definitive method for playing. It's offered humbly as a starting point for empowering you to discover for yourself what works and what doesn't.

I sincerely hope this handbook proves to be an invaluable guide in your journey toward becoming a better guitar player.

—Luke Zecchin

Introduction

What is great guitar technique? An overly simple yet fitting definition of technique is our ability to maximize *tone* while minimizing *tension*. That is, we want to play with fluency, clarity, and accuracy in a way that feels comfortable and natural. This principle underpins everything covered in this book.

Admittedly, differences in body type, playing style, personal preference, and other variables make it difficult to define a one-size-fits-all approach to playing technique. The simple truth is that different people do things differently. Proper playing technique isn't defined by whether it's right or wrong, but by whether it's working. In other words, is it an approach to playing that produces the desired result? Technique doesn't exist for its own sake; it exists to help us do things better, in ways that are easier.

We often assume that technique means finding the correct way to do something. While there's truth to this, it can lead to thinking that *correct* technique is some kind of foreign ideal to be attained. Something that's somehow different from what feels natural or intuitive. But think about it: Isn't playing in a way that feels natural and intuitive the end goal? There's no doubt that learning to play well involves developing new skills. However, it's the bad habits we learn along the way (usually without realizing it) that slow progress and hinder the effectiveness of our playing. Often, good technique is defined less by what we need to learn and more by what we need to *relearn*.

Ideally, we want playing guitar to feel as effortless as possible. Because we tend to make things more difficult than they need to be, we'll quickly discover that *effortlessness* requires practice. The intention of this book is to give you clear reference points for evaluating and improving your own playing technique. We'll discuss foundational concepts, take a detailed look at various playing mechanics, and introduce specific exercises for increased accuracy, speed, and endurance.

A key concept we'll revisit is establishing a comfortable home base, or default position to reference when playing. In programming our body to recognize the feeling of good technique, we train ourselves to better diagnose when we're playing in ways that are unhelpful and counterproductive. The more we cultivate good playing habits, the more we'll find that these occur naturally when playing.

Great technique means being mindful of the things we do that inhibit great playing. It's not about doing what we think is correct or what we see others do. It's about doing what works. (Hint: If it's uncomfortable or painful, it's not working!) Trial, error, and experimentation are always our greatest teachers. As we learn to get out of the way of our own playing, we'll experience greater control, fluency, and freedom.

1

Fundamental Concepts

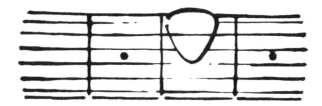

Before looking at the specific mechanics of playing technique, let's establish some general ground rules for this discussion.

Play It Comfortably

Have you ever wondered how great performers make playing music look effortless? At first this seems counterintuitive to what you might expect. After all, common logic usually assumes that the harder something is, the harder we have to try. For example, picture a professional athlete in the heat of battle. You wouldn't exactly call that *effortless*. Even extraordinary effort, however, can be characterized by a necessary degree of effortlessness. Think about the impeccable technique, free-flowing movements, clear thinking, and natural instinct needed to compete at the highest level. If an athlete were to tense up all their muscles, contort their body into a strange position, and hold their breath, how well do you think they'd perform?

Amazingly, this is what many guitar players do as soon as they start playing! They tense up their arms and shoulders, clench their jaw, hunch awkwardly over the guitar, and even hold their breath to concentrate. Perhaps more surprising is the lack of awareness that these things are happening at all. If we consistently place ourselves in difficult playing conditions, is it any wonder why playing feels so difficult?

Despite these tendencies, the body is most effective when it's comfortable, relaxed, and able to move freely. Nothing is more counterproductive to effective technique than making your body work against itself. Doing so expends unnecessary energy and produces unnecessary tension. Notice that the term just used was *unnecessary* tension. Tension in itself isn't a bad thing. We couldn't even hold the guitar, let alone play it, if our muscles didn't use some tension to expand and contract. Unnecessary tension is the excess stress we place on our body that doesn't need to be there. It's caused by things like poor body position, moving inefficiently, overworking muscles, and forgetting to breathe.

Smooth, relaxed movements are far more conducive to accuracy, speed, and endurance than tense, rigid ones. This is a central concept we'll revisit continually. Your body will tell you if it's tense or uncomfortable—listen to it. Playing *naturally* takes practice. It means learning to be aware of your body when you play, your general tendencies, your bad habits, and your specific idiosyncrasies. It means constantly reminding yourself to breathe normally, stay relaxed, and move comfortably. Great performers make complex things look effortless because they've learned to play complex things *effortlessly*.

Play It Accurately

What makes a skilled musician so captivating? Even though we may admire a performer's command of their instrument, we often praise them for their artistry, paying little attention to their technical proficiency. When was the last time you walked away from a concert commenting on the artist's impressive *finger dexterity* and notable *fine motor skills*? Although these mechanical elements may not be the first things we think of, they're as much responsible for a musician's ability as their musicality or creativity. Artistry goes hand in hand with execution.

You don't have to be a virtuoso to work out the simple equation: Poor execution equals poor performance. Consistent issues with intonation, lack of clear sustain, unwanted string noise, and excessive fret buzz are typical hallmarks of poor playing technique. These things can plague both beginners and relatively experienced players alike. Unfortunately, even a potential masterpiece won't equate to much if we can't translate it from our mind to our fingers.

Proper execution involves maneuvering your fingers with control and accuracy. It means getting them to do exactly what you want. Inaccurate playing is often the result of ineffective playing habits such as glossing over issues, forgetting to relax, and being inattentive to detail. These problems, however, are usually traced back to a common root cause: *practicing things too fast*. Attempting to play something faster than we're capable is counterproductive. It teaches us to practice mistakes, causes our movements to stiffen, and doesn't allow for the precision needed to learn something effectively.

Accuracy starts with two key things. First, knowing what you want to achieve. And second, knowing how to get there. When you slow something down enough to play it perfectly (often much slower than you assume), you give yourself the opportunity to isolate issues and then correct them. This process is fundamental to what practice essentially is: *problem-solving*. It's about finding the roadblocks between where you are and where you want to go, and then working out how to overcome them.

Playing slowly allows you to play *intentionally*. It enhances your awareness, letting you focus on your body, your technique, and your tone. It gives you the opportunity to program good playing habits, instead of unintentionally learning bad ones. Of course, this doesn't mean that playing fast should be avoided. It's a simple reminder that walking always comes before running. The first step in learning to play fast is learning to play slow. Increasing speed comes easily once you've removed the barriers holding you back.

Play It Efficiently

How do we get the most from our technique with the least amount of effort? This question underpins our entire discussion on playing technique. There's no benefit in unnecessary effort. It increases the stress on your body and decreases the stamina of your playing. Consider the difference between a person who touch-types fluently and one who punches the keyboard awkwardly using their index fingers. One moves quickly with minimal effort. The other progresses slowly, flapping their hands wildly. Which technique is more effective and sustainable?

Economy of motion is a pivotal concept in effective technique. Even playing something comfortably and accurately at a slow tempo doesn't mean you're playing it *efficiently*. Try progressing slowly through a scale while moving your hand away from the guitar neck and relaxing your arm between each note. This is probably comfortable and possibly even accurate, but it's not very effective. A focus on efficiency dictates how our movements can be used most effectively to achieve the best results. Playing slowly isn't the goal—it's the process, the method through which we program our body to make relaxed and efficient movements.

In contrast, we tend to exaggerate our movements when learning because it emphasizes the important information. For example, think about how we sound out unfamiliar words to small children or use animated hand gestures to give directions on the street. For guitar players, these exaggerated movements are usually compounded by the tendency to tense up and apply too much pressure when playing. Learning to minimize motion (e.g., the distance our fingers travel from the fretboard or our pick's proximity to the strings) avoids overemphasizing the actual movement required by either hand. *Economizing* our technique in this way makes playing easier, more controlled, and can dramatically improve our playing speed.

Playing efficiently doesn't mean making your movements more timid—just more condensed. After some practice, you may be surprised at how little motion is needed to maintain clear tone, dynamics, and expression. Cultivating efficient technique is one of the most valuable skills you have in unlocking your playing potential. *Streamlined motion* is the secret component behind many great players. It minimizes tension, improves accuracy, increases speed, and maximizes endurance. As the saying goes, *Why work harder when you can work smarter?*

Play It Freely

What makes a great performance? Think of a time when you *really* wanted to play well. Perhaps an important gig, an audition, a recording session, or just the first time you played in front of someone else. How did it go? Did the need to sound good produce great playing, or did it cause you to overthink and underperform? Most people find that the pressure to play well diminishes their ability to do so. Why? Because when performing, we often become overly fixated on the outcome, the gripping desire to be perceived a certain way. Ironically, this need to sound good is often what gets in the way of actually sounding good!

Contrast this with our mentality when practicing. In the process of learning and improving, we give ourselves permission to play, experiment, and make mistakes. In other words, we're far less attached to the outcome because we're absorbed in the *process*. Admittedly, the goal of practice is different to that of performance. Practice focuses on weaknesses; performance relies on strengths. One requires concentrated observation and critique, while the other requires spontaneity and lack of inhibition. The point is, in practice we need to build control–in performance we need to *surrender* it.

Ideally, practice should be where we do all our thinking so it doesn't distract us in performance. With that said, developing great technique is also a *circular* process. You need good technique to play freely, but as just discussed, you also need to play freely to have good technique. Sounds contradictory, right? If one doesn't exist without the other, where do we start? The answer begins with simply acknowledging this fact. The goal of practice isn't to increase the complexity of our playing; it's to make complex things increasingly easier. Our focus shouldn't be on needing to play well or sounding good, but on wanting to play *freely*. Mastery comes from continually removing the things that inhibit our musicality. As we learn to play with greater freedom (both in our technique and in our thinking), sounding good takes care of itself.

This says a lot about how we should approach learning. We've established that the pressure caused by our inner critic often hinders performance. If our internal dialogue impacts our playing ability, why are we so quick to reinforce those assertions that impede our progress? If we constantly tell ourselves that something is *too difficult*, for example, is it any surprise that we usually prove ourselves right?

Playing with freedom means adjusting our mindset to believe that difficult things can be done with great ease, and then slowly convincing our fingers to cooperate. Always start with the question: What would this look, sound, and feel like if I could already do it?

2

Playing Position

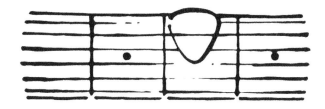

Having introduced some key concepts, let's begin by exploring how our playing position is foundational to everything we do on guitar.

Body Position

It's a fair assumption that most people have some idea about the impact of poor posture on the body. We're usually reminded of this when we sit or stand in the same position for too long. It's interesting how many of the positions we initially define as *relaxed* often become uncomfortable when held for an extended time. This is especially true when an activity requires the skill and concentration involved in playing an instrument.

From a young age, many of us would be familiar with the common instruction to *stop slouching and stand up straight*! The problem is that body tension caused by trying to maintain good posture can be as unhelpful as body tension caused by not trying at all. That is, we often respond by overarching the spine, pulling our shoulders back, and pushing our chest out—stiffening like a soldier standing at attention. How comfortable is that after a few minutes?

It's difficult to have a natural playing technique when we're forcing our body into an unnatural position. Effective technique works with the body, not against it. It seeks to execute complex movements in the simplest, most efficient way possible. This begins with first establishing a comfortable foundation, or *home base*, for our body. We can explore this with the following simple exercise.

Finding Your Default

Find a comfortable chair that's not too high and is relatively firm. Sit down, placing your feet flat on the ground, and slide up to the front half of the seat. Rotate your pelvis forward slightly to rest on your *sit bones* (the two large bones that connect with the chair; picture how a cellist sits). Next, relax your neck and allow your head to rotate forward and up, as if being gently guided away from the top of the spine by an imaginary string. Now, balancing your head comfortably on top of your neck, take a deep breath, and exhale slowly, letting your shoulders rest evenly above your ribcage.

What do you notice about the position of your body?

- First, sitting forward on a comfortable but supportive chair (not slumped into a couch) allows the sit bones to feel like they're plugged securely into the seat. You're not arching back or hunching over. Instead, the weight of your body should feel centered and stable.

- Next, you should notice a gentle curve in your lower back, lengthening the torso and letting the shoulders sit level. Note that this isn't about pushing your chest out or pulling your shoulders back. It's about staying positioned naturally, without trying too hard.

- Last, you might experience a slight floating sensation as your neck relaxes and allows the head to balance comfortably. Notice that your chin isn't slanting upward or being pulled inward, and the back of your head isn't compressed down on the neck. Focus on the sensation of length, width, and openness in your body.

Internalize this feeling. This is what we'll call our *default* body position. By this we mean it's the position where our body feels both supported and comfortable. Being mindful of your body position (and the bad habits you fall into) ensures that your body isn't working against itself when playing guitar. Unnecessary tension in the back, shoulders, and neck caused by hunching over or sitting awkwardly will affect the speed, fluidity, and endurance of your playing technique.

Remember, the way we use our body is a choice. Because we often forget to make good choices with posture and body position, it may take some practice before this becomes habit. Fortunately, developing technique isn't a race. We're setting ourselves up for success over the long term. Even seemingly small adjustments, practiced regularly, can have a big impact over the life of your playing.

Playing Mechanics

Sit or Stand?

Let's look closer at the specifics of playing position. First, the position of your guitar will have a notable impact on your technique. One obvious question before even picking up the guitar is: Should we sit or stand to play? The answer is *both*. While you may have a particular preference, you'll likely be required to do both in different situations. Knowing this, let's briefly cover some common problems to look for in each scenario.

When sitting down to play, there's less potential for the guitar to move, which usually feels more stable. However, our body position will shift inconsistently depending on the chair being used (e.g., consider the significant height difference between a piano stool and a bar stool). Additionally, the guitar is often not placed centrally to our body, forcing the guitar neck to sit relatively horizontal, angling away from us. This can position our torso awkwardly and make it harder for our left hand to navigate the lower frets. These issues are often compounded by a tendency to slouch back into the chair or hunch over the guitar body.

Example 2.1

Alternatively, when we're standing, the guitar naturally hangs more central to our body. However, the benefit of this is counterbalanced by our shoulder now becoming responsible for the full weight of the guitar. Not only can this affect posture and shoulder tension, but it also becomes more physically demanding the longer we play. Having the guitar at an adjustable height can also be problematic. Hanging the guitar too low (despite its popularity in the '90s) angles the wrists unnaturally and makes it much harder to play.

Example 2.2

Playing Position

Having already established our default body position, we now have a reference point for positioning the guitar. Remember, the goal is comfortable movement, stability, and freedom from excess tension. Ideally, the guitar should be positioned centrally to our body. Although the guitar is commonly placed over the right leg when sitting, as highlighted, this flattens the guitar neck horizontally and pushes it diagonally across our body. In turn, this often results in twisting the torso and angling the shoulders to accommodate.

Instead, borrowing from our classical brothers and sisters, a preferable alternative when practicing is to position the guitar centrally over the *left* leg. This rotates the guitar to be flatter across our body, allowing our arms, shoulders, and torso to sit more naturally. The guitar can then be angled slightly in toward our torso for full view of the fretboard without hunching over. Note that it isn't necessary to hold the guitar in place. It should rest naturally, secured by its various points of contact with the body. You'll also notice that classical guitarists will often elevate their left leg. This ensures the guitar neck tilts up comfortably for easier access, raising the headstock above shoulder height. While footstools are less common in mainstream genres, a similar effect can be achieved by tucking the right foot in toward the chair and dropping the right leg.

Example 2.3

Allowing the guitar to complement our default body position when sitting also provides a useful reference point when standing. If we adjust our guitar strap from this sitting position (softer, wider straps provide the best support), we're able to keep the guitar in a consistent position. This limits the number of variables that can impact technique when our playing position changes. It also ensures that the guitar always remains at a comfortable height, letting the arms hang naturally and keeping both wrists relatively straight.

Example 2.4

Whether sitting or standing, the neck and shoulders are a common source of tension for guitar players. This is often compounded by a tendency to tense, raise, or drop either shoulder while playing. Our default body position reminds us that stability, width, and openness across our shoulders is key. When moving your left hand, it's important to pivot primarily from the elbow, not the shoulder. Your arm should fall naturally next to your side, ensuring the elbow isn't tucked in tightly against your body or angled out awkwardly. Likewise, your right shoulder should remain balanced with the left, not lifted up or hunched down. Finally, it's also good to be conscious of how often you look down at the fretboard. You'll notice that most players constantly have their necks kinked without even realizing it (usually out of habit, not necessity).

Summary

We commonly change the position of our body to accommodate the position of the guitar. Given that the guitar doesn't care what position it's in nearly as much as our bodies do, this makes no sense! Instead, allowing the guitar to align comfortably with how we want to position our body is the central concept here.

This doesn't mean that we should never move from one set position. Although it might be easier playing in the same environment, under the same conditions, using the same chair, with the same equipment—this isn't realistic. For most musicians, whether you're jamming with friends, moving around on stage, or sitting in the studio, your body will need to navigate many playing situations. Ultimately, learning to play comfortably in various settings is the end goal.

Notice that I've repeatedly used the term *default* to describe our playing position. It's simply intended as a reference point. The takeaway is that we want to program our body to recognize the feeling of good technique. This trains us to better diagnose how it feels when we're falling into bad habits or playing in ways that are counterproductive. The more we cultivate good playing habits, the more we'll gravitate to them naturally, regardless of the playing situation.

Let's recap the key ideas:

- **Be Mindful of Posture:** Slouching and staying relaxed aren't the same thing! It's very difficult to keep tension out of your body if you sit awkwardly or hunch over while playing. Effective body position is the foundation of effective technique.

- **Avoid Over-Correcting:** Good posture feels *good*; it shouldn't feel forced. We should be gently lengthening our body from the top of the spine, letting the neck, shoulders, and torso rest naturally. The experience of comfortably supporting the body compared with overworking it is very different.

- **Keep the Guitar Central:** The way we position the guitar will dictate how we position our body. Placing the guitar centrally aligns it more comfortably with the natural position of our body and allows for free movement in both arms.

- **Elevate the Headstock:** The guitar neck should tilt up diagonally at a comfortable angle. Positioning the neck too horizontally can obstruct the natural movement of the left arm and create unnecessary tension in the wrist.

- **Make the Height Consistent:** Ideally, the guitar should stay at approximately the same height whether sitting or standing. This avoids hanging the guitar too low, putting excess strain on the arms and wrists, and keeps our playing technique more consistent in either situation.

Exercise 1

Capture a short video of yourself practicing to observe your current playing technique.

Set up a camera, smartphone, or tablet in your usual practice space. (If this isn't possible, a similar exercise can be done with a mirror.) Record roughly 3-5 minutes of yourself playing guitar. The quality of the footage isn't important, as long as you can see yourself clearly on playback.

Play through whichever song, exercise, or technique you're currently working on (preferably something that requires enough focus to help you forget you're being filmed). Don't think about the position of your body or the guitar; just practice like you usually would. The idea is to capture an accurate snapshot of yourself in a normal playing situation. To help with this, it may be useful to repeat this exercise a few times from different angles (e.g., front-on and side-on).

Next, put down the guitar and review the footage. Pay close attention to the position of your body when playing. What do you notice?

- Are your neck and shoulders resting comfortably, or are they hunched over the guitar?

- Do your shoulders stay relatively level, or does one bunch up higher than the other?

- Does your left arm fall naturally, or is your elbow crammed up against your body or angled out awkwardly?

- Is your right arm moving comfortably, or is it tense and rigid?

- Does your torso complement the natural curve of your spine, or is your chest collapsed?

- How does your body position shift between the beginning and end of the video as you became less conscious of being filmed?

- Do you change your playing position during the more difficult parts of the song or exercise?

- How do external factors like the strap you're using, the chair you're sitting on, or the position of the guitar itself seem to affect your technique?

These types of questions help you observe the nuances of your own playing technique. Try to connect this visual feedback with the sensation you experience in your body when playing. Are there any specific tension areas you notice: your neck, shoulders, forearms, etc.? If so, can you notice anything about your current technique that might contribute to this?

The goal here is simple. In establishing *good* playing habits, we're also reprogramming *bad* ones. It's very hard to solve a problem we can't identify. The ability to assess our technique objectively often highlights various unhelpful tendencies that go unnoticed because we've learned to experience them as normal.

Exercise 2

Before practicing, take a moment to prepare yourself for playing. Sit with the guitar, focus your attention, and relax.

Often, we're already tense even before picking up the guitar. Instead of launching into that latest song or riff, simply take a moment to practice sitting (or standing). Think about the position of your guitar and the position of your body. Shift into the default playing position where your body feels centered and comfortable. Without playing, hold this position and slowly count to 10. Shut your eyes and use this time to scan your entire body for tension. Take a few deep breaths and consciously relax.

For at least the first few weeks, regularly reassess your body position when practicing (e.g., every 5 minutes or before each new exercise). Having used the previous exercise to identify any unhelpful tendencies, be particularly mindful of those. This is especially true when doing something challenging that requires more concentration. If you notice old habits creeping back into your playing, avoid getting frustrated, reset your default position, and continue playing.

As a greater awareness of your playing technique develops, continue to reference this exercise when practicing. At casual intervals, consciously gather a mental snapshot of your playing position. Scan your body for tension, recenter yourself, relax, and then carry on.

Extra Credit

- It's helpful to repeat **Exercise 1** multiple times. Try to review new footage of yourself playing every 2-3 weeks, over the course of a few months. Use this visual feedback to isolate any ongoing problems and track your development.

- Try repeating **Exercise 1** in an alternate playing situation. If you usually practice sitting, do this exercise standing, or vice versa. What differences can you observe in your playing position? Does this highlight anything new to be mindful of when playing?

3

Left-Hand Technique

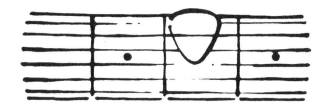

*Now that we've established a firm foundation, let's move forward with a detailed look
at the specifics of left-hand technique.*

Left-Hand Position

The left hand is responsible for the melodic content we play on guitar. Interestingly, the first place many students learn to maneuver their left hand is actually the most difficult. It's logical that the best position to start would be at the 1st fret, right? The guitar is tuned to the open strings, it's the easiest place to memorize note names, and most songs for beginners use open chords around this position. While this is all true, it's also the furthest stretch from our body where the frets are the greatest distance apart.

Beginning around this position moves our hand away from our body, often angling the wrist and causing us to push down harder than necessary. Put simply, learning to play where the left hand is the least comfortable creates the greatest potential for tension. Because we often focus more on the notes being played than on the hand playing them, we learn to interpret this feeling of excess tension as normal. Is it any wonder why seeing the pros play effortlessly at almost unintelligible speeds seems so baffling?

The habits we learn early on become the framework for everything we do on guitar. It's very difficult to cultivate playing speed and fluid movement when our basic technique works against us. To play freely with minimal tension, we need to revisit the fundamentals of left-hand technique. Let's explore this with the following simple exercise.

Finding Your Default

Drop your left hand next to your side and relax your arm. Gently shake out any tension and let your thumb and fingers fall naturally toward the floor. Next, keeping your arm relaxed, maintain the exact position your fingers are in but rotate your palm to face forward. Now, pivoting from the elbow, bring your hand up as though you're holding an imaginary guitar neck.

What do you notice about the position of your hand?

- First, the wrist stays relatively straight. It isn't tilted out to either side or bending awkwardly. It sits comfortably in the middle of its radius.

- Next, the thumb is positioned upright. It isn't sticking out horizontally or folding in across the palm. It falls naturally in parallel with the 1st finger.

- Last, the fingers sit upright while still maintaining their natural curve. They aren't being held together tightly, flattened out, or stretched apart. They're positioned naturally, with a comfortable space between each finger.

This is your *default* left-hand position. It's the position in which your wrist, thumb, and fingers are most comfortable. As such, this position enables you to maximize the accuracy and speed of your left hand. Why? Because the more we minimize unnecessary tension in the left hand, the less resistance it will encounter. (This concept should sound familiar by now.) For example, try bending your wrist up at a 90° angle and then wiggle your fingers. How comfortable is it to move them freely compared to when your wrist is straight? Not comfortable at all! Amazingly, this type of exaggerated hand position is relatively common among guitar players.

As with our discussion on playing position, finding your default left-hand position doesn't mean your hand must stay like this at all times. Naturally, the left hand needs to move dynamically in response to the particular things being played on the fretboard. It simply means that this is the position we should revert back to and seek to maintain when possible.

Left-Hand Mechanics

The Thumb

Let's look closer at the specifics of left-hand technique. In establishing our default position, we discovered that the thumb should sit upright across from the 1st finger. The idea is to create equal pressure between the thumb and fingers, much like a gentle vice. If we bend the thumb out horizontally (toward the guitar headstock) it will impact the stability of our grip. If we angle the thumb in across the palm (toward the 4th finger) it will increase tension in the thumb and palm while playing.

Generally, the thumb should pivot comfortably behind the middle of the guitar neck, on or slightly to either side of where the neck-curve is at its thickest. Raising the thumb too high over the neck can cause our palm to wedge up against the fretboard, impacting the mobility and natural curve of our fingers. Dropping it too low can increase the angle of our wrist, adding unnecessary tension and resistance in our movement. Good thumb position enables the wrist to stay straight, leaving the palm relatively parallel to the guitar neck with a comfortable air gap in between.

Example 3.1

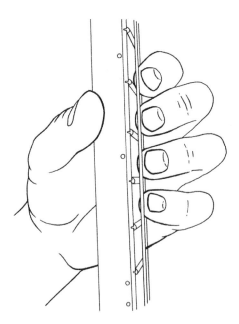

Note that the thumb is used only for stability; its role is to guide and steady. To do this, it needs to shift freely in parallel with the fingers. Think of the thumb and fingers as one cohesive unit maneuvering together. The pressure applied to the strings comes primarily from the natural weight of the arm, not from over-clamping the thumb. In fact, we should be able to lift the thumb from the guitar neck completely and still hear notes sustain clearly. While this exercise doesn't make for great playing technique, it's a good indicator of whether we're relying too much on pressure from the thumb.

As mentioned already, the left hand should move naturally in response to what's being played. At times, the thumb might come up over the fretboard to keep the wrist straight when playing open chords or to add leverage when bending strings. At other times, it may lean out horizontally when reaching for higher frets or to let the fingers angle diagonally for larger stretches, and so on. These types of intuitive movements are necessary to make playing easier. The point is, for general playing, the default position is our reference for comfortable and effective technique.

The Fingers

In observing the natural orientation of our fingers, we found that they curve in, staying relatively parallel with the frets and allowing space between each finger. Like the hammers in a piano, it's important that our fingers move back and forth freely with minimal resistance. If we hold our fingers too tightly together, stretch them too far apart, or angle them unnecessarily, it can hamper the speed and efficiency of our movements.

Keeping with the image of piano hammers, our hands should contact the strings accurately, using the tips of our fingers. If we play using the pads of our fingers, it flattens them out, causing clumsy or unintentional contact with the strings. (The obvious exception is using a barre to fret multiple notes at once.) Given its natural curve, each finger will connect with the strings at a slightly different angle. However, for minimal buzz and intonation issues, aim for the same point of contact on every fret. In general, always target the front half of a fret but ensure that your finger stays clearly behind the fret wire.

Example 3.2

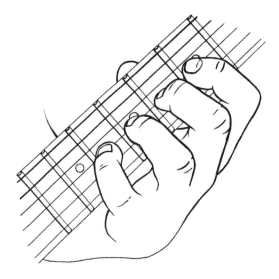

A common issue for guitar players is pressing too hard on the strings. Many don't realize how little pressure is needed to sound a note cleanly. Keep in mind that we're only pressing the string down against the *fret wire*, not the actual fretboard. This distance is much smaller than people often assume. Playing with more pressure than required slows down your technique, causes excess tension in the hand, and often results in intonation problems. Consider for a moment your natural finger dexterity. Most people can tap their fingers quickly with relative ease when sitting at their desk. Why do we assume that playing guitar requires significantly more effort? We're essentially using the same movements.

Another common cause of inefficient left-hand technique is lifting fingers too far away from the fretboard (especially the 4th finger). The principle here is simple: If you halve the distance of your fingers from the strings, you halve the time they take to play a note. Notice that as our fingers relax, they lift up naturally. When a finger releases a note, it doesn't need to be *pulled* up from the fretboard; the movement is part of its natural motion. This issue is also connected with pressing too hard. When our fingers travel further than necessary, they'll usually hit their destination with more force than necessary. Keeping our fingers as close as possible to the strings (without interfering with them, of course) will maximize the speed and fluidity of our left hand by minimizing the movement required.

Summary

When thinking about left-hand technique, it's easy to compartmentalize things. The angle of your wrist, the position of your thumb, the movement of your fingers, and so on. Even though it's easier to explain and demonstrate these things in isolation, in reality this isn't how they function. Everything is connected. The reason these things are important is because they affect one another. The angle of your wrist and the position of your thumb directly impact the mobility of your fingers, and vice versa. Good technique moves intuitively as needed but exerts no more effort than required.

Let's recap the key ideas:

- **Keep Your Wrist Straight:** Your wrists are most comfortable in the middle of their radius. Keeping your wrist relatively in line with the forearm (a slight incline is normal) will reduce stress on the joint and enable your fingers to move freely with minimal resistance.

- **Monitor Your Thumb Position:** Ideally, for general playing, your thumb should sit upright, positioned comfortably behind the guitar neck across from your 1st finger. Poor thumb position can affect the stability, natural curve, and mobility of your fingers.

- **Use Your Fingertips:** Unless you're holding down multiple strings at once, avoid playing with the pads of your fingers. Allow each finger to angle in comfortably (keeping with its natural curve) and contact the strings using only your fingertips. Focus on accuracy and control.

- **Gauge Your Pressure:** It's often surprising how little pressure is needed to sound a note cleanly. Remember, there's only a small distance between the bottom of a string and the top of a fret. Decreasing excess pressure will increase your speed and agility.

- **Keep Your Fingers Close:** The further your fingers travel back and forth from the strings while playing, the more unnecessary effort you expend. Minimizing these movements will maximize the efficiency of your left hand, resulting in a lighter touch and a faster technique.

Exercise 3

Using a basic chromatic exercise, practice squeezing and releasing notes to accurately gauge left-hand pressure.

Starting on the low E string, rest your 1st finger above the 7th fret. Lightly press the bottom of the string to the top of the fret wire. Do this softly and slowly; you should not hear any sound. Repeat this multiple times, gently releasing the string from the fret and then pressing it down again. Keep your hand relaxed but avoid lifting your finger off the string. Notice how little pressure is actually required to move the string.

Next, remaining on the low E string, move to the 8th fret with your 2nd finger and repeat this exercise. Focus on the lightness of your touch and avoid using more pressure than necessary. Complete the exercise with your 3rd and 4th fingers, ascending one fret for each finger:

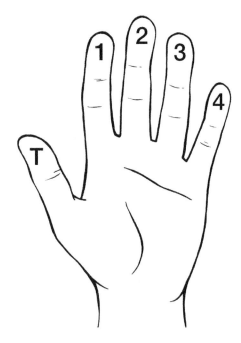

Continue this exercise across all six strings, starting from the 7th fret on each string:

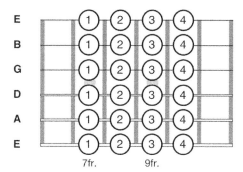

Now, repeat the exercise again, this time including your picking hand. At a slow tempo, play through each note several times using alternate downstrokes/upstrokes. When a finger rests on the string, the picked sound should be dull and muted. As it slowly pushes down to the fret, there should be a series of buzzy, ugly-sounding strokes. Finally, as the string transitions to proper contact with the fret, the note will sound cleanly, with no buzz.

Once each note rings clearly, hold it for a few seconds, taking care not to apply any further pressure. Capture a mental snapshot of how little tension is needed to play notes across multiple strings, using different fingers. When this feels natural, maintain the sensation of lightness in your left hand and practice cycling through each four-fret chromatic sequence normally, without first needing to gauge your pressure.

Exercise 4

Using a series of diagonal notes on the fretboard, practice finger independence and controlled motion.

Starting on the A string, rest your 1st finger above the 7th fret. Place your other fingers diagonally across the D, G, and B strings. As with the previous exercise, each finger should be assigned its own fret (all a half step apart). Make sure your fingers rest lightly on top of each string, without pressing down:

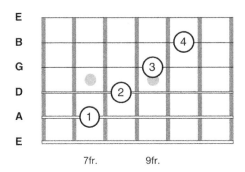

Begin with your 1st finger and play a note, applying the minimum pressure needed. Pick the note cleanly and then release it, cutting short the sustain. To do this, relax your finger but don't lift it from the string; you should not hear any additional ringing. Repeat this several times, ensuring that your hand stays relaxed. Try to keep your other three fingers resting diagonally on their subsequent strings, *without* moving.

Next, leave your 1st finger resting on the A string and repeat this exercise with your 2nd finger (on the 8th fret of the D string). Remember, the central idea is to keep your other three fingers in place, resting on each string but not pressing down. This is an exercise in control and economy of motion. The point is to move each finger independently without affecting the others. Complete this exercise using your 3rd and 4th fingers. Although it may seem simple, this is deceptively difficult and takes practice.

Now, repeat this exercise again but *invert* the shape of your fingers to slope in the opposite direction. In other words, they should rest diagonally from the 4th finger (on the 10th fret of the A string) to the 1st finger (on the 7th fret of the B string):

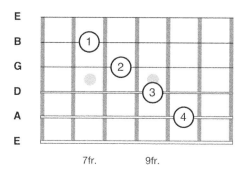

Developing control and independence in your left hand takes time. Be sure to go slowly and stay relaxed.

Extra Credit

- Experiment with the method for gauging pressure in **Exercise 3**, but this time apply it to different fretboard patterns. Practice playing through familiar scale or arpeggio shapes, remaining conscious of the pressure and tension in your left hand.

- Apply the idea of control and economy of motion (demonstrated in **Exercise 4**) to the ascending chromatic sequence outlined in **Exercise 3**. Using the same four-fret pattern across all strings, this time leave your fingers planted down after each note has been played. Release each finger only when it moves across to the next string. Again, this can be deceptively difficult, so be sure to take it slowly.

4

Right-Hand Technique

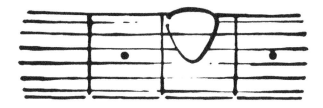

Finally, having looked at playing position and left-hand mechanics, this section concludes with an in-depth discussion on right-hand technique.

Right-Hand Position

An effective picking technique is vital for any great guitar player. A lack of precision and control won't affect only the speed of your playing but also your tone, timing, and dynamics. Although it's easy to focus on the acrobatics of the left hand, the right hand is the central component in both rhythm and sound production. Developing a reliable and efficient picking technique will be one of your most valuable assets in playing guitar.

In the mechanics of picking technique, there are several variables. These include the type of guitar pick used, how it's positioned against the strings, and the preferred picking motion. While these are all important aspects of right-hand technique, the fundamental starting point is how we hold the pick to begin with. Keeping the pick secure while minimizing tension in the right hand, wrist, and forearm is essential. Let's explore this with the following exercise.

Finding Your Default

Drop your right hand next to your side and relax your arm. Gently shake out any tension and let your thumb and fingers fall naturally. Next, keeping your elbow at your side, bring your forearm out straight and let your fingers dangle freely with your palm facing the floor. Now, stay relaxed but rotate your palm to face the ceiling, letting your fingers and thumb come together naturally.

What do you notice about the position of your hand?

- First, like your left hand, the wrist stays relatively straight. It's not angled up or down or bent awkwardly to one side. It sits in the middle of its radius, allowing for free movement.

- Next, the thumb falls comfortably alongside your index finger. It's not sticking upright away from the palm. It rests relatively flat, aligning with your wrist and forearm.

- Last, all four fingers come together, curling in naturally toward the palm. They aren't being held out straight or clenched into a tight fist. Instead, they rest comfortably.

Keeping your hand in this position, slide the guitar pick between your thumb and the side of your index finger (with the point facing up to the ceiling). You've now found your *default* right-hand position. This is the position in which your wrist, thumb, and fingers feel most relaxed when using a pick.

In placing the guitar pick, be sure to hold it firmly but not tightly. Your picking hand should feel stable, not tense. A common problem is leaving too much of the pick exposed. Instead, the majority of the pick should be placed securely between your thumb and index finger. No more than the top third should be visible (often much less for faster picking). This minimizes the tension needed to hold the pick securely and results in more controlled picking strokes.

Example 4.1

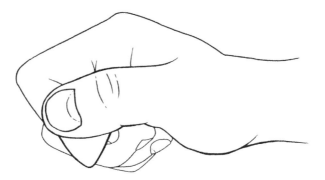

Admittedly, more so than with the left hand, right-hand technique varies widely among guitar players. A slight variation to this position (and one I use personally) places the guitar pick similar to how you might hold a pen or pencil when writing. In this scenario, the pick is positioned more between the thumb and the pad of the index finger (the side of the middle finger can also be used for extra support). Compared with the original position, each finger tends to open out a little more while still maintaining its natural curve.

Example 4.2

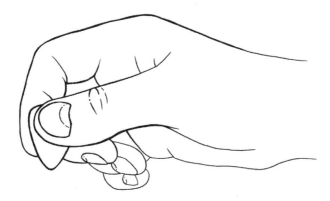

Ultimately, the exact picking technique you adopt is a matter of preference based on what feels most natural. The important thing is that your pick should feel stable, and your hand should feel relaxed. Notice that, in either example, the primary job of your fingers is to hold the pick securely. They're not responsible for the actual picking motion. This movement is generated from larger mechanics in the right arm (as discussed in the next section). Again, as with every other aspect of playing technique, minimizing unnecessary work maximizes the speed and efficiency of your movements.

Right-Hand Mechanics

The Pick

Let's look closer at the specifics of right-hand technique. Having established how to hold the pick, we'll now discuss how to use it effectively. First, the shape and thickness of your guitar pick will have a noticeable impact on your playing. Typically, thicker picks (e.g., 1–3mm) with a sharper point produce better results for lead playing. On the other hand, thinner picks (e.g., 0.60–0.90mm) with a rounder point are usually more comfortable for rhythm playing. The logic here is simple: The more rigid the pick, the more precision and control you have; the more pointed the pick, the less resistance it encounters from the strings.

Example 4.3

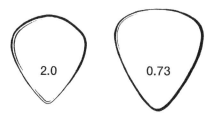

Your choice of guitar pick should come down to the preferred sound and feel for whatever style you're playing. However, there are other variables to consider. Sound-wise, the angle of your pick when it strikes a string alters the presence or attack of the note. Similarly, the distance you pick from the guitar bridge also influences the bite or roundness of your tone. Beyond these tonal preferences, the way your pick is used also affects the accuracy and speed of your technique. When strumming, as long as the pick is secure, the specifics of your technique will have less impact on your playing. When picking, though, the importance of your technique is magnified proportionally to the precision and control you're trying to achieve.

Generally, strumming requires more flexibility from your pick. Because this movement involves less precision and more force, keeping the pick rigid is less beneficial. For faster lead playing, however, stability is key. To maximize accuracy and speed, tilt your pick at approximately a 45° angle to the strings (so the pick is angled *edge-first*). The direction of this tilt depends on your technique for holding the guitar pick. Most players find that the pick slopes down naturally toward their left foot, although some find it more comfortable angled back toward their right foot. Beyond increasing the attack of each stroke, using the edge of the pick also creates less resistance against the strings. This means it stays placed more securely without slipping.

Example 4.4

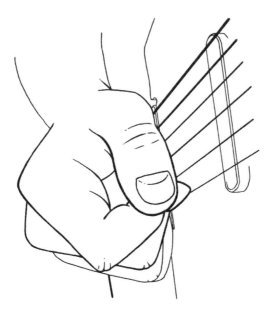

As with the left hand, keeping your guitar pick close to the strings will maximize the speed and efficiency of your technique. The shorter the distance you move past the string on a downstroke, the less you have to come back on an upstroke. Picture each string as having a magnetic pull that keeps your pick in almost constant contact. Don't move through the string—stay connected *to* the string. Making contact with only the tip of your pick, you may be surprised at how little movement is necessary. Done properly, your pick should feel controlled and stable in relation to the string.

For faster picking, it's beneficial to consider the slant of your guitar pick when alternating strings. Picking with a faint upward/outward motion (depending on the stroke direction) means that instead of running clumsily into the next string, the pick ends up just above it. This puts the pick in a better position for the next upstroke or downstroke. Put simply, we're picking with a slight diagonal motion as opposed to moving perfectly flat across the strings. While this seems like a minor technicality, picking with precision and speed requires very nuanced movements. Fortunately, players often gravitate toward these things intuitively the more they focus on accuracy and efficiency.

The Arm

In discussing picking technique, it's helpful to first break down the basic mechanics of *strumming*. When we strum through a chord progression, our right arm is responsible for the percussive and rhythmic elements of our playing. Just like a drummer hitting a snare, the hand, wrist, forearm, and elbow should all function as one cohesive unit. Rather than being tense or rigid, all parts of the arm need to move intuitively with one another to work effectively.

There are a number of basic variables when strumming: the position of the guitar, the rhythm being played, the tempo of the music, and so on. To successfully navigate these while still playing in time, the right arm needs to move freely, distributing the work naturally across its various components in coordination. The elbow generates momentum, the forearm rotates naturally to position the hand, and the wrist articulates the attack of each strum. In contrast, playing only from the elbow would make for an extremely rigid performance, while moving only from the wrist would be tiring and very ineffective.

This is useful for understanding the mechanics of picking technique. We should view the hand, wrist, forearm, and elbow as one unit, working together. As with strumming, relying only on momentum generated from a single part of the arm could cause it to become stressed and overworked. Remember, vibrating a guitar string requires very little motion. Unlike strumming, however, when picking these movements are significantly more nuanced and less noticeable.

To demonstrate this concept, try playing a basic strumming pattern over a simple chord progression. As you play, gradually make your strumming motion smaller and smaller. Keeping your arm relaxed, slowly condense this movement until you end up playing just one string (aim for one of the middle strings). Now, let your forearm rest comfortably on the guitar body with your wrist settling gently over the guitar bridge. Ideally, your wrist should stay relatively straight while still able to move freely. Your forearm should coordinate naturally with these movements while stabilizing your arm on the guitar. And your elbow should be able to pivot your hand comfortably from string to string as needed. Notice that using your elbow to pivot between strings keeps the picking motion consistent, maintains the pick's angle to each string, and avoids excessive bending in the wrist.

Additionally, it's common to use one or more loose fingers to stabilize your right hand against the guitar body. However, you should avoid sticking the index, ring, or pinky fingers out straight (so they're pushing firmly against the guitar). Instead, keep them relaxed and let them curl in naturally, resting on or just below the high E string. Another popular *anchoring* technique involves resting the fleshy part of your palm where the low strings meet the bridge. This is preferable for muting notes or taming unwanted noise from surrounding strings. Always remember, when you're only playing one string, there are five others you don't want to hear!

Summary

Picking technique can vary widely among guitar players. Even the same player may use different approaches, depending on what they're playing. Despite these variations, the general principles are likely to remain the same. *Relaxed, efficient movements are good; tense, rigid movements are not.* We often assume that developing speed in our technique comes from making our movements faster. However, speed is more accurately seen as a byproduct of making our movements smaller and more economical. Ironically, in learning to use less effort, we begin seeing greater results.

Let's recap the key ideas:

- **Choose Your Pick:** The shape and thickness of your guitar pick impacts both technique and tone. Thicker, pointed picks are generally used for increased precision and control. Thinner, rounder picks are usually preferable for less intricate movements, like rhythm playing.

- **Tilt the Pick 45°:** There's less resistance in your picking technique when the pick is positioned at a slight but consistent angle to the strings (not flat or parallel). Positioning the guitar pick flat causes it to move more, reducing its stability and resulting in less control.

- **Focus on Efficiency:** Pick using only the tip of your guitar pick, holding it securely but not tightly for smooth and controlled strokes. Focus on staying connected to the string, minimizing your picking motion to increase speed and efficiency.

- **Work as a Unit:** Effective picking technique is the result of various components in the arm working together intuitively. Overworking a single part, such as the wrist or elbow, is likely to cause unnecessary issues. Excessive stress is the enemy of speed and fluidity.

- **Anchor Your Hand:** Keep your arm in constant contact with the guitar. Resting your forearm, palm, or fingers gently on the guitar provides greater stability in your picking technique. This is essential for maintaining controlled and accurate movements.

Exercise 5

Using a single string, practice the feeling of efficient picking technique at fast tempos.

Mute all six strings by resting your left hand across them without pressing down. Begin by slowly picking alternate strokes on the muted B string. Keep each stroke slow and wide, exaggerating these up and down movements so your pick almost touches the E and G strings on either side.

Gradually increase the speed of your picking motion. As you do this, start to minimize the distance your pick moves past the muted B string on each stroke. Remember to keep your right hand positioned properly, with the pick secure and your arm relaxed. Play using only the tip of the guitar pick to avoid catching too much of it on the string.

Slowly accelerate to a top speed that's comfortable, continuing to minimize your picking motion as you do so. Picture the pick as connected securely to the string. Ensuring each stroke remains clear and consistent, try to make the pick appear as if it's hardly moving. (If things sound choppy or unsteady, you're trying to play too fast.) Once you've reached your peak tempo, decrease your picking speed again and return to the slow, wide strokes you started with. Repeat this exercise several times, looping steadily between slow and fast, wide and narrow.

Once comfortable, do this exercise again but let the B string ring open (still keeping the other strings muted). Again, cycle from slow to fast picking strokes, economizing your movement as the speed increases. For added stability, try muting the B string slightly with the fleshy part of your palm. Make sure each note remains clear and consistent. Notice how the sound and feel changes as your picking motion condenses. Focus on the contrast between these movements and the impact picking efficiency has on playing speed.

Exercise 6

Using a single string, practice the feeling of efficient picking technique at slow tempos.

Set a metronome to a slow tempo that's comfortable (no faster than 60 BPM). Begin by picking quarter notes (one note per beat) on the open B string using alternate strokes. The goal is to exaggerate efficient motion by making each note as short as possible. Importantly, this exercise doesn't involve the left hand. Instead, you must cut each note short using *only* your guitar pick. To do this, strike the string with one side of your pick and then immediately stop it with the other. As the pick stops the string from ringing out, it will create a short, muted stab (or *staccato*) sound. Done properly, this should feel like one fluid movement.

By limiting the follow-through of your picking action, you begin consciously economizing your movement. Once this action feels natural, stay at the same tempo but increase the rhythm to 8th notes (two notes per beat). As with the previous exercise, you may find it helpful to mute the B string slightly with the fleshy part of your palm. Next, continue cutting off each stroke into short stabs and move to playing triplets (three notes per beat), followed by 16th notes (four notes per beat). Finally, when comfortable, try moving to 16th-note triplets (six notes per beat).

When you can play each rhythm at a consistent tempo, begin looping them. Start with two bars of quarter notes, progressing to two bars of 8th notes, then triplets, and so on. Once you've played through each rhythm, return to quarter notes and continue cycling through. As the rhythm changes, be sure to focus on the consistency and timing of each muted stab.

Note: This is purely an exercise in economy of motion; the point is to accentuate the feeling of efficient picking. Practicing fast and efficient movements at slow tempos is extremely beneficial for developing control and playing speed.

Extra Credit

- Practice **Exercise 5** across all six strings, using both open strings and fretted notes. Try to maintain your top tempo for increasingly longer periods. At your peak tempo, see if you can switch dynamically between playing loud and soft while still keeping the speed consistent.

- Practice **Exercise 6** across all six strings, using both open strings and fretted notes. When comfortable at slower tempos, incrementally increase the speed of this exercise. For example, each time a new tempo feels natural, try speeding up the metronome by 5 BPM.

Final Thoughts

Congratulations on completing **Total Guitar Technique**!

This handbook was written for those looking to develop greater control, speed, and endurance in their guitar playing. The intention wasn't to overload you with complex exercises or grueling practice routines. Instead, we've focused on the essentials of what great technique looks and feels like. All the songs, exercises, licks, and playing tricks in the world are of little benefit if your foundational technique works against you!

The goal of this book has been to provide a detailed breakdown of the mechanics involved in guitar playing. We've then outlined clear and practical starting points to experiment with these yourself. You needn't be overwhelmed by this detailed exploration into playing technique. Remember, great playing arises from the desire to create great music. Technique is simply the thing we develop along the way to help us do this better. It's cultivated over time in the continual process of learning, revisiting, experimenting, and tweaking.

Ultimately, despite its complexities, playing music is still just *playing*. There's no rulebook! The simple takeaway is to be mindful of what your body is telling you. Great technique starts with recognizing where you're getting in the way of your own playing. Navigating bad playing habits is a normal part of learning. The problem isn't that they occur but that they often happen without us knowing (until they're so obvious, we're forced to pay attention!).

In the introduction, I stated that good technique is often defined less by the things we need to learn, and more by the things we need to *relearn*. Notice that the term used was relearn, not *unlearn*. The focus isn't on undoing bad habits; it's on cultivating new ones. This process is as much a change in mindset as it is technique. Framing things negatively only slows progress by increasing frustration. Instead, when you focus on the solutions, the problems tend to take care of themselves.

May this book help inspire you toward continued learning and creativity.

Appendix | Guitar Mechanics

Whether your guitar is worth $300 or $3000, having it set up properly is essential. A guitar that's not correctly adjusted makes it harder to distinguish between issues with your technique and issues with your instrument. In short, it's difficult to play effortlessly if you're fighting your instrument the whole way! You don't have to be a luthier to get the most from your guitar, but it's important to be aware of common problem areas. Guitar maintenance involves more than just changing strings every so often. Basic adjustments to the guitar neck, string height, and intonation will have a notable impact on your technique, tuning, and tone.

Learning to recognize the sound and feel of potential issues ensures that your instrument doesn't interfere with your playing. You may have heard it said, *A poor craftsman blames his tools*. Perhaps a better sentiment is that a true craftsman never gives himself a reason to blame his tools. Although each guitar is different, below is a brief overview of some key things to be mindful of.

Note: If you're uncertain how to adjust your guitar properly, be sure to get it serviced by an experienced guitar tech.

Neck Curve

To compensate for movement, guitar necks have a metal truss rod running through their center. The tension of this truss rod varies the neck between two general positions. If it's too tight, the neck will bow outward (toward the strings). If it's too loose, the neck will bow inward (away from the strings). Neither extreme is ideal. If the neck bows out too much, it interferes with the natural vibration of the strings, resulting in excessive fret buzz and a lack of clear sustain. If the neck bows in too much, it creates tuning issues and becomes harder to play around the middle of the fretboard. Generally, it's preferable to have the guitar neck set relatively straight, with a small amount of *relief*. This means keeping a slight natural curve to compensate for the midpoint where strings vibrate the most.

Action & String Gauge

The height of the guitar strings relative to the fretboard will greatly impact a guitar's playability. If the action of the strings is too high, the guitar becomes difficult to play and is prone to intonation problems. If the action is too low, there'll be excessive fret buzz and notes won't sustain clearly. These issues can be corrected at the guitar bridge. Setting the exact string height is largely a matter of preference, but it's also affected by your choice of string gauge. Lighter strings are easier to press down and require less pressure to bend. However, they're often considered to have a thinner, less desirable tone. In contrast, heavier strings usually provide a fuller, louder sound and allow for a lower action. However, the increase in tension means they require more effort to play. Fortunately, the various thicknesses available make it easy to find a comfortable match for your setup preferences and playing style.

Intonation & Tuning

For a guitar to be relatively in tune across the whole fretboard, the 12th fret must be the tonal center point for each string. Setting the intonation at the guitar bridge alters the string length to compensate for this. When this adjustment is off, a string won't align properly with its tonal center point. If the string length is too long, notes will sound flatter as you move up the guitar neck. If the string length is too short, notes will sound sharper. While it may seem logical to set the bridge consistently across all strings, intonation is calibrated by a string's pitch, not its length. This means that the bridge must be adjusted to compensate for the variables of each individual string. These include the curve of the guitar neck, the radius of the fretboard, the tension of the string, and the string's proximity to the frets.

Nut, Frets & Bridge

When you're playing, the nut, frets, and bridge are all critical points of contact with the guitar strings. Over time, these surfaces are susceptible to general wear and tear. If any of the nut slots, fret wires, or bridge saddles develop inconsistencies or become overly worn, they'll likely cause issues with intonation, fret buzz, and string breakage. Alternatively, if the nut or bridge of the guitar have never been adjusted properly (even if the guitar is brand-new), they'll often increase playing difficulty and cause tuning issues. It's important to be aware of the impact these key factors have on the tone and playability of your guitar.

Liked This Book?

Did you find this book useful? You can make a big difference in helping us spread the word!

While it would be nice to have the promotional muscle of a major publishing house, independent authors rely heavily on the loyalty of their audience. Online reviews are one of the most powerful tools we have for getting attention and finding new readers.

If you found this book helpful, please consider helping us by leaving an online review at your place of purchase. Reviews needn't be long or in-depth; a star rating with a short comment is perfect. If you could take a minute to leave your feedback, it would be sincerely appreciated!

Additional Resources

For more resources, including great free content, be sure to visit us at:

www.guitariq.com

Stay in touch with all the latest news. To connect with us online, head to:

www.guitariq.com/connect

Would you like to read more? For a complete list of Luke's books, check out:

www.guitariq.com/books

Remember to grab your online bonus! Get the free bonus content for this book at:

www.guitariq.com/tgt-bonus

Interested in a master class with Luke? To check out his online workshops, go to:

www.guitariq.com/academy

About the Author

Having played for over 25 years, Luke Zecchin is an accomplished guitarist with a wealth of studio and live experience. Outside his work teaching music, Luke has toured extensively alongside renowned national and international acts, performing at everything from clubs, theaters, and festivals to various appearances on commercial radio and national television.

Playing lead guitar, Luke has worked on projects with established international producers and engineers. He has been fortunate to see these collaborations break into both the Top 50 ARIA Album and Singles charts, having also received nationwide airplay and notable debuts on the Australian iTunes Rock charts.

As the founder of **GuitarIQ.com**, Luke is dedicated to the education and coaching of guitar players all over the globe. With books available in over 100 countries worldwide, he has emerged as an international chart-topping author in his field.

Luke continues to work as an author and musician from his project studio based in the Adelaide Hills, South Australia.

Find him online at **LukeZecchin.com**.

Printed in Great Britain
by Amazon